AF444318

This book is dedicated to everyone who has ever had trouble explaining the way they feel. It's hard sometimes, but we can figure it out together.

-P.D.

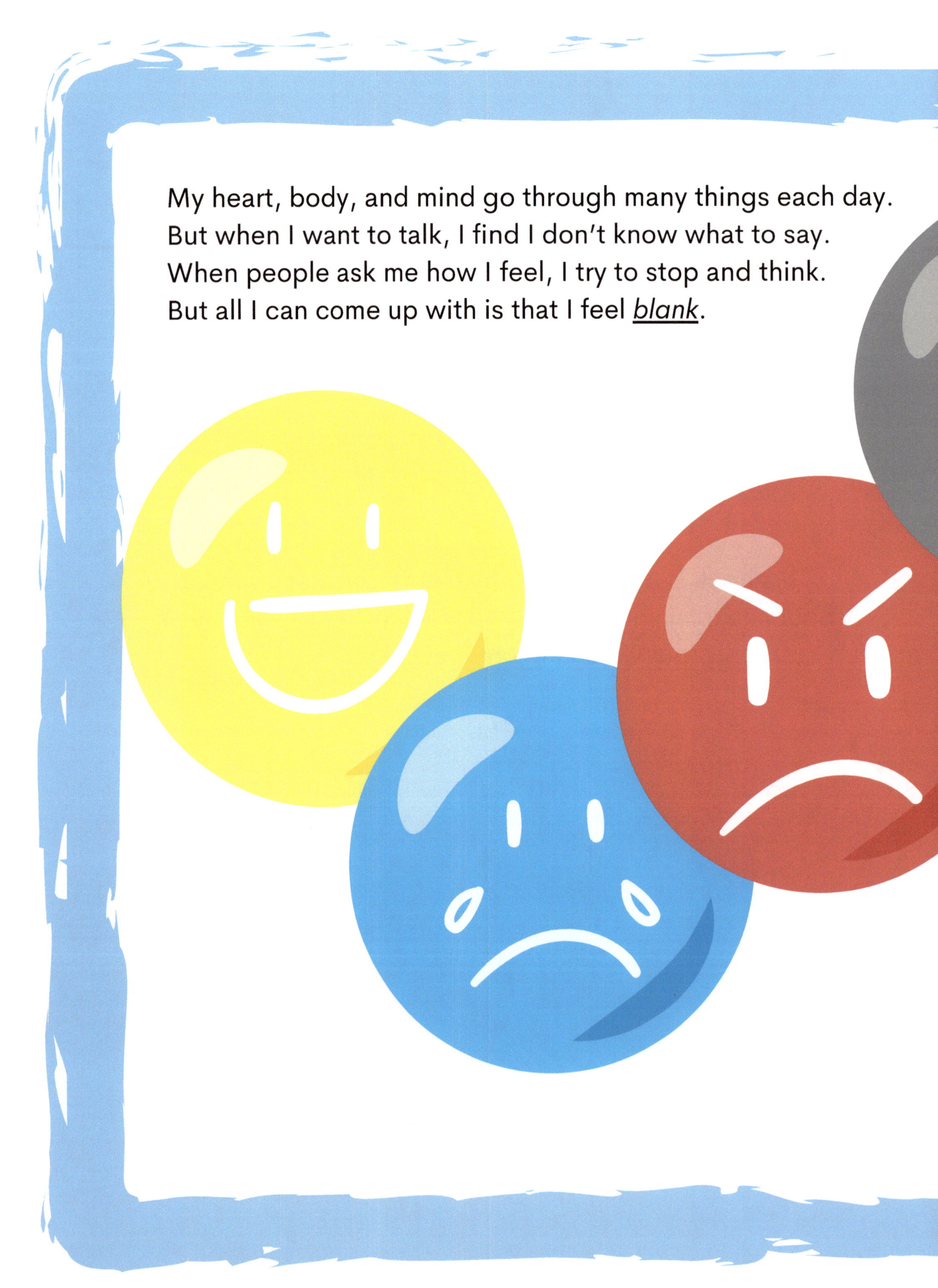

My heart, body, and mind go through many things each day.
But when I want to talk, I find I don't know what to say.
When people ask me how I feel, I try to stop and think.
But all I can come up with is that I feel _blank_.

A _blank_ is where a word should go but I don't know them all.
want to learn some words to name my feelings, BIG and small!

I love the times when I can smile and laugh and play and sing.
I want to tell the world out loud! I want to make bells ring!
This feeling makes my heart so warm, you see it on my face.
I want to always feel this way, I'm in my smiley place.

lovely

content

joyful

happy

cheerful

pleased

glad

Who do I tell? What do I say? It's hard to stop and think.
There must be something better than "I feel _blank_."

Other times when something comes along and breaks my heart.
I feel my body droop and then my smile falls apart.
Sometimes I even cry out loud where everyone can hear,
Especially when I lose someone or something I hold dear.

Who do I tell? What do I say? It's hard to stop and think.
There must be something better than "I feel _blank_."

When things don't go the way I want, my tummy starts to turn.
My shoulders tense, I grit my teeth, my ears and face might burn
And sometimes, if it's really bad, my body starts to shake.
That is when I know for sure I need to take a break.

AGGRAVATED

FURIOUS

ANGRY

MAD

UPSET

IRRITATED

FRUSTRATED

Who do I tell? What do I say? It's hard to stop and think. There must be something better than "I feel _blank_."

sleepy

drowsy

drained

worn out

sluggish

exhausted

tired

I want to keep on going, because playing is the best!
But after playing all day long, I have to take a rest.
My eyes get heavy, I slow down, and I begin to yawn.
The longer I let this feeling build, I know I can't go on.

Who do I tell? What do I say? It's hard to stop and think.
There must be something better than "I feel _blank_."

Oh no! I feel my heart race and I want to run away!
Something loud or big or painful makes me feel this way.
I wish someone would hold me tight and tell me I'm okay.
Most times I think I'm pretty brave, but maybe not today.

TERRIFIED

PANICKED

FEARFUL

ALARMED

FRIGHTENED

SCARED

AFRAID

**Who do I tell? What do I say? It's hard to stop and think.
There must be something better than "I feel _blank_."**

quiet

bashful   nervous

embarrassed

ashamed   alone

shy

I feel so many eyes on me. I want to hide my face.
I'd rather whisper than talk out loud, so please give me my space
My face is red again and I kind of want to cry.
But I'm not sad, I'm just not ready, and I do not know why.

Who do I tell? What do I say? It's hard to stop and think.
There must be something better than "I feel _blank_."

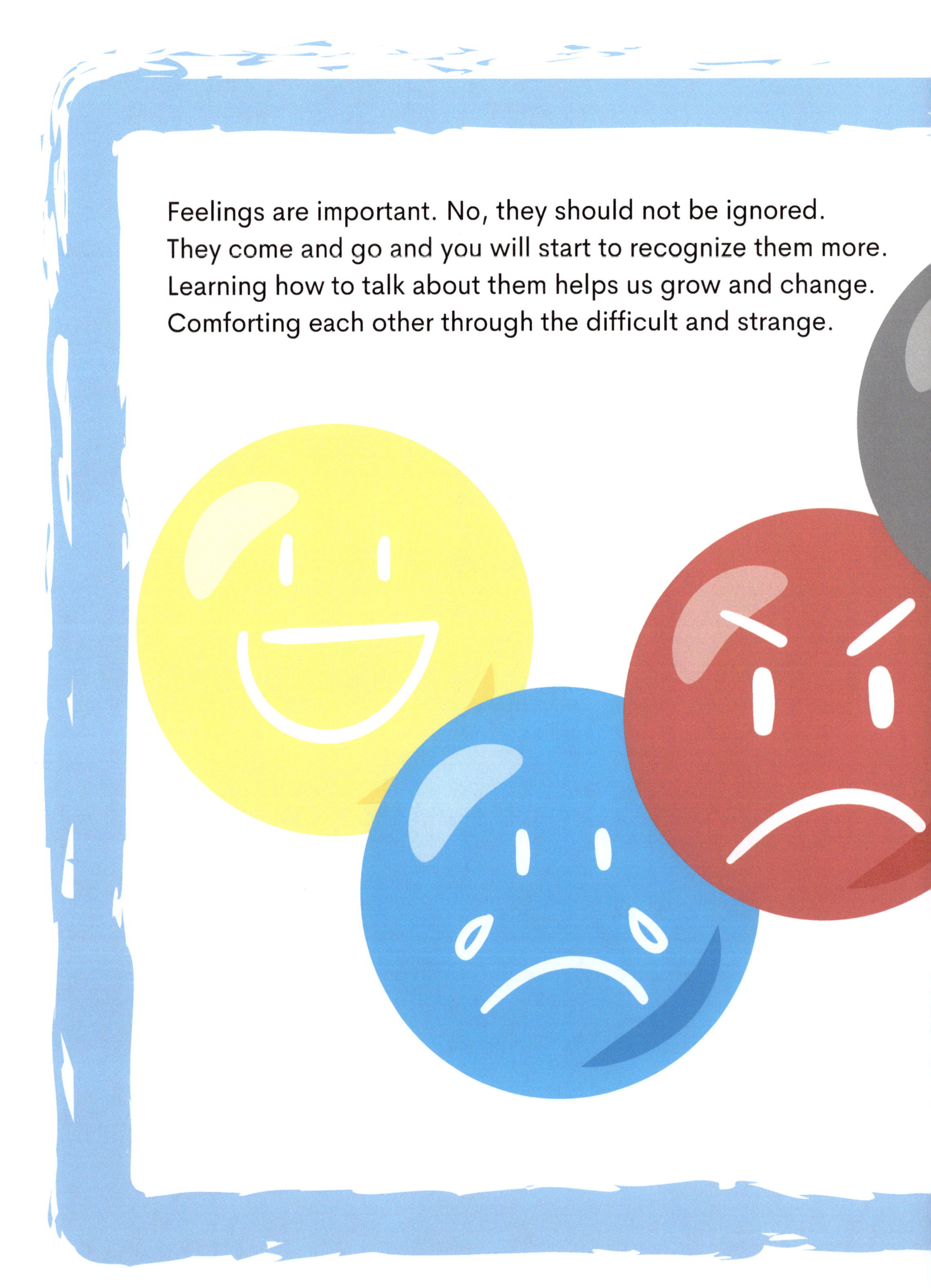

Feelings are important. No, they should not be ignored.
They come and go and you will start to recognize them more.
Learning how to talk about them helps us grow and change.
Comforting each other through the difficult and strange.

So when you get a feeling that is just too strong to hold,
Use these words and share them. Be loud, be brave, be bold.
It's true sometimes, when feelings hit, it's hard to stop and think.
But now we know what words are better than "I feel _blank_!"